Cute Crochet Baby Clothes Patterns To Try

Sophia R. Hughes

All rights reserved. Copyright © 2023 Sophia R. Hughes

COPYRIGHT © 2023 Sophia R. Hughes

All rights reserved.

No part of this book must be reproduced, stored in a retrieval system, or shared by any means, electronic, mechanical, photocopying, recording, or otherwise, without written permission from the publisher.

Every precaution has been taken in the preparation of this book; still the publisher and author assume no responsibility for errors or omissions. Nor do they assume any liability for damages resulting from the use of the information contained herein.

Legal Notice:

This book is copyright protected and is only meant for your individual use. You are not allowed to amend, distribute, sell, use, quote or paraphrase any of its part without the written consent of the author or publisher.

Introduction

Welcome to this book, a collection of adorable and charming patterns that will warm the hearts of both babies and their loved ones. In this guide, we will explore the world of baby crochet, where creativity meets coziness, and where handmade creations become treasured heirlooms.

We begin our journey with baby hats, the perfect accessory to keep little heads snug and stylish. From delicate bonnets to playful animal-inspired designs, you'll find a variety of patterns that cater to different tastes and skill levels. These baby hats are not only functional but also serve as adorable fashion statements, making them the perfect gift for newborns and infants.

Moving on, we dive into the realm of baby sweaters, where warmth and cuteness come together. Our collection features a range of sweater patterns, from simple and classic designs to more intricate and decorative styles. These cozy garments will keep babies snug and stylish, showcasing your crochet skills while creating lasting memories for both the wearer and the maker.

No baby ensemble is complete without a pair of booties. Our bootie patterns will guide you through creating tiny footwear that is not only adorable but also comfortable for little feet. Whether you prefer classic designs or more whimsical motifs, you'll find patterns that capture the essence of baby cuteness while ensuring a cozy fit.

Each pattern in "Lovely Baby Crochet Patterns" is thoughtfully designed with love and care, incorporating a combination of stitches, colors, and embellishments to create one-of-a-kind pieces. The patterns cater to various skill levels, allowing beginners to embark on their crochet journey and experienced crafters to expand their repertoire.

Crocheting for babies offers a unique opportunity to create meaningful gifts and keepsakes. Handmade items carry a special touch and are infused with love, making them cherished treasures for both parents and little ones. With this book, you'll be able to craft beautiful garments and accessories that will be treasured for years to come.

So, gather your crochet hooks, soft yarn, and a sprinkle of creativity as we embark on a delightful journey through the world of baby crochet. Whether you're creating gifts for your own little ones or making heartfelt presents for others, the patterns in this guide will inspire you to bring joy, warmth, and a touch of handmade love to the sweetest souls in our lives.

Get ready to crochet lovely baby hats, adorable sweaters, and tiny booties that will make hearts melt and create lasting memories. Let's begin this heartwarming adventure with this book.

Contents

Baby Hats 1

Baby Sweaters 27

Booties 66

BABY HATS

Wrapped With Love Preemie Crochet Hat

Crochet Hook H/8 or 5 mm hook

Yarn Weight (4) Medium Weight/Worsted Weight and Aran (16-20 stitches to 4 inches)

Crochet Gauge In hdc, 15 stitches and 12 rows = 4" (10 cm)

Finished Size Preemie

Materials List

Worsted weight yarn such as Caron Simply Soft in Color A and Color B

5.0 mm (H-8) crochet hook or size needed to obtain the gauge

Yarn needle for weaving in ends

Preemie Hat Pattern:

Special Instructions:

The hat can be started with a Magic Ring or with the instructions given in Round 1

The beginning chain does not count as a stitch

Each round is started in the same stitch as your beginning chain

The end of each round is joined by slip stitching in the first stitch of the round, not the beginning chain

Size 1 - 2 Pounds

Head Circumference = 8" - 10"

Hat Circumference = 8"

Height hat = 3.65"

Round 1: With Color A - Ch 2, work 9 hdc into the 2nd chain from the hook, join in first hdc (9)

Round 2: Ch 1, make 2 hdc in each stitch around, join (18)

Round 3: Ch 1, *make 2 hdc in first stitch, hdc in next* repeat around, join (27)

Round 4: Ch 1, *make 2 hdc in first stitch, hdc in next 8 stitches* repeat around, join (30)

Round 5 - 6: Ch 1, hdc around, join (30)

Change to Color B

Round 7 - 8: Ch 1, hdc around, join (30)

Change to Color A

Round 9 - 10: Ch 1, hdc around, join (30)

Round 11: Ch 1, sc around, join (30)

Fasten off and weave in all ends.

Size 2 - 3 Pounds

Head Circumference = 9" - 11"

Hat Circumference = 9"

Hat Height = 4"

Round 1: With Color A - Ch 2, work 9 hdc into the 2nd chain from the hook, join in first hdc (9)

Round 2: Ch 1, make 2 hdc in each stitch around, join (18)

Round 3: Ch 1, *make 2 hdc in first stitch, hdc in next stitch* repeat around, join (27)

Round 4: Ch 1, hdc in first 3 stitches, *make 2 hdc in next stitch, hdc in next 3 stitches* repeat around, join (33)

Round 5 - 7: Ch 1, hdc around, join (33)

Change to Color B

Round 8 - 9: Ch 1, hdc around, join (33)

Change to Color A

Round 10 - 11: Ch 1, hdc around, join (33)

Round 12: Ch 1, sc around, join (33)

Fasten off and weave in all ends.

Size 4 - 5 lbs

Head Circumference = 10" - 12"

Hat Circumference = 9.75"

Hat Height = 4.5"

Round 1: With Color A - Ch 2, work 9 hdc into the 2nd chain from the hook, join in first hdc (9)

Round 2: Ch 1, make 2 hdc in each stitch around, join (18)

Round 3: Ch 1, *make 2 hdc in first stitch, hdc in next stitch* repeat around, join (27)

Round 4: Ch 1, *make 2 hdc in first stitch, hdc in next 2 stitches* repeat around, join (36)

Round 5 - 8: Ch 1, hdc around, join (36)

Change to Color B

Round 9 - 10: Ch 1, hdc around, join (36)

Change to Color A

Round 11 - 13: Ch 1, hdc around, join (36)

Round 14: Ch 1, sc around, join (36)

Fasten off and weave in all ends.

Bow

With Color B

Round 1: Ch 3, into 1st chain make *1 dc, 3 tr, 1 dc, ch 2, sl st in same ch*, ch 2, repeat between *, fasten off

Fasten off leaving a long tail. Use the tail to wrap the center of the bow a few times. Secure the ends and use the longer tail to sew the bow onto the hat. I used it to secure each end of the bow so it doesn't curl up.

The Parker Crochet Baby Hat

Materials:

–Lion Brand Vanna's Choice yarn (Weight: 4/Medium, 3.5 oz/100g, 170 yds/156 m)

(*You will use less than half a skein for any size of this pattern*)

–Size H 5mm crochet hook (*click here to see my favorite one!*)

–Tapestry needle

–Scissors

Shop my favorite tools & materials here!

Sizes:

0-3 months, 3-6 months, 6-9 months, 9-12 months, toddler/preschooler, child

Gauge:

14 sts x 8 rows in dc = 4"

Skill Level:

Level 1/Beginner

Notes:

-Sizing is based on the Craft Yarn Council sizing guide – you can view that here.

-Make sure you check your gauge via the measurements above to be sure your hat fits the child you're making it for perfectly.

-View the video tutorial here.

0-3 Months

Crochet Baby Hat

Magic ring, 11 DC in magic ring, join to first DC, chain 2

Round 2: 2 DC around, join, chain 2 (22)

Round 3: 2 DC in first, DC in next; repeat around, join, chain 2 (33)

Round 4: 2 DC in first, DC in next 2, repeat around, join, chain 2 (44)

Rounds 5-7: DC around, join, chain 2 (44)

Rounds 8-10: DC in first, FpDc in next, repeat around, join, chain 2 (44)

Round 11: Sc around, join, finish off (44)

3-6 Months

Crochet Baby Hat

Magic ring, 11 DC in magic ring, join to first DC, chain 2

Round 2: 2 DC around, join, chain 2 (22)

Round 3: 2 DC in first, DC in next, repeat around, join, chain 2 (33)

Round 4: 2 DC in first, DC in next 2, repeat around, join, chain 2 (44)

Round 5: 2 DC in first, DC in next 10, repeat around, join, chain 2 (48)

Rounds 6-8: DC around, join, chain 2 (48)

Rounds 9-11: DC in first, FpDc in next, repeat around, join, chain 2 (48)

Round 12: Sc around, join, finish off (48)

6-9 Months

Crochet Baby Hat

Magic ring, 11 DC in magic ring, join to first DC, chain 2

Round 2: 2 DC around, join, chain 2 (22)

Round 3: 2 DC in first, DC in next, repeat around, join, chain 2 (33)

Round 4: 2 DC in first, DC in next 2, repeat around, join, chain 2 (44)

Round 5: 2 DC in first, DC in next 10, repeat around, join, chain 2 (48)

Round 6: 2 DC in first, DC in next 11, join, chain 2 (52)

Rounds 7-9: DC around, join, chain 2 (52)

Rounds 10-12: DC in first, FpDc in next, repeat around, join, chain 2 (52)

Round 13: Sc around, join, finish off (52)

9-12 Months

Crochet Baby Hat

Magic ring, 11 DC in magic ring, join to first DC, chain 2

Round 2: 2 DC around, join, chain 2 (22)

Round 3: 2 DC in first, DC in next, repeat around, join, chain 2 (33)

Round 4: 2 DC in first, DC in next 2, repeat around, join, chain 2 (44)

Round 5: 2 DC in first, DC in next 10, repeat around, join, chain 2 (48)

Round 6: 2 DC in first, DC in next 11, join, chain 2 (52)

Round 7: 2 DC in first, DC in next 12, join, chain 2 (56)

Rounds 8-10: DC around, join, chain 2 (56)

Rounds 10-13: DC in first, FpDc in next, repeat around, join, chain 2 (56)

Round 14: Sc around, join, finish off (56)

Toddler / Preschooler

Crochet Hat

Magic ring, 11 DC in magic ring, join to first DC, chain 2

Round 2: 2 DC around, join, chain 2 (22)

Round 3: 2 DC in first, DC in next, repeat around, join, chain 2 (33)

Round 4: 2 DC in first, DC in next 2, repeat around, join, chain 2 (44)

Round 5: 2 DC in first, DC in next 10, repeat around, join, chain 2 (48)

Round 6: 2 DC in first, DC in next 11, join, chain 2 (52)

Round 7: 2 DC in first, DC in next 12, join, chain 2 (56)

Round 8: 2 DC in first, DC in next 13, join, chain 2 (60)

Rounds 9-11: DC around, join, chain 2 (60)

Rounds 12-14: DC in first, FpDc in next, repeat around, join, chain 2 (60)

Round 15: Sc around, join, finish off (60)

Child

Crochet Hat

Magic ring, 11 DC in magic ring, join to first DC, chain 2

Round 2: 2 DC around, join, chain 2 (22)

Round 3: 2 DC in first, DC in next, repeat around, join, chain 2 (33)

Round 4: 2 DC in first, DC in next 2, repeat around, join, chain 2 (44)

Round 5: 2 DC in first, DC in next 10, repeat around, join, chain 2 (48)

Round 6: 2 DC in first, DC in next 11, join, chain 2 (52)

Round 7: 2 DC in first, DC in next 12, join, chain 2 (56)

Round 8: 2 DC in first, DC in next 13, join, chain 2 (60)

Round 9: 2 DC in first, DC in next 14, join, chain 2 (64)

Rounds 10-12: DC around, join, chain 2 (64)

Rounds 12-15: DC in first, FpDc in next, repeat around, join, chain 2 (64)

Round 16: Sc around, join, finish off (64)

Abbreviations (US Terms):

ch – chain

dc – double crochet

sc – single crochet

Baby Elephant Crochet Hat

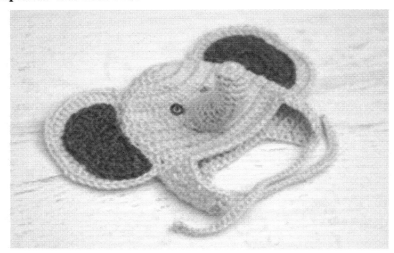

Crochet Hook H/8 or 5 mm hook

Yarn Weight (4) Medium Weight/Worsted Weight and Aran (16-20 stitches to 4 inches)

Materials List

Lion Brand Heartland Yarn in Katmai and Olympic

Size H Crochet Hook

Tapestry needle

Black buttons for eyes (or you could crochet eyes)

Poly-fil stuffing for trunk

Hat Pattern

Main Body

Magic Ring, chain 2 and make 11 DC inside ring, join to first DC, chain 2

Round 2: 2 DC in each stitch around, join, chain 2 (22 DC)

Round 3: 2 DC in first stitch, DC in next stitch, join, chain 2 (33 DC)

Round 4: 2 DC in first stitch, DC in next 2 stitches, join, chain 2 (44 DC)

Rounds 5-9: DC in each stitch around, join, chain 1 (44 DC)

Round 10: SC in each stitch around, join (44 SC)

Continue on earflaps or fasten off and leave hat without earflaps

Earflap 1

Chain 1, SC in next 10, chain 1, turn

Row 2: SC decrease, SC in next 6, SC decrease, chain 1, turn

Row 3: SC across (8 SC)

Row 4: SC decrease, SC in next 4, SC decrease, chain 1, turn

Row 5: SC across (6 SC)

Row 6: SC decrease, SC in next 2, SC decrease, chain 1, turn

Row 7: SC across (4 SC)

Row 8: Make 2 SC decreases, chain 1, turn

Row 9: SC decrease, fasten off, weave in ends

Earflap 2

Leave 16 stitches along the front of hat...

Join yarn, chain 1, SC in next 10, chain 1, turn

Row 2: SC decrease, SC in next 6, SC decrease, chain 1, turn

Row 3: SC across (8 SC)

Row 4: SC decrease, SC in next 4, SC decrease, chain 1, turn

Row 5: SC across (6 SC)

Row 6: SC decrease, SC in next 2, SC decrease, chain 1, turn

Row 7: SC across (4 SC)

Row 8: Make 2 SC decreases, chain 1, turn

Row 9: SC decrease, and continue to SC around hat and earflaps, when you get to the top of each earflap: chain 35, slip stitch in 2nd chain from hook and the rest of the way down the chain. Continue to SC around the hat and fasten off when you get the entire way around.

Left Ear

Magic Ring, chain 2 and make 8 DC in ring, pull tight but do not join. You should have a half circle, chain 2, turn

Row 2: 2 DC in each stitch, chain 2, turn (16 DC)

Row 3: 2 DC in first stitch, DC in next, repeat till end, chain 2, turn (24 DC)

14

Row 4: [2 DC in first stitch, DC in next 2] (4x), 2 SC, SC in next 2, *2 DC, DC in next 2, repeat from * until end. Fasten off leaving long tail.

Inside Left Ear

Magic Ring, chain 2 and make 8 DC in ring, pull tight but do not join. You should have a half circle, chain 2, turn

Row 2: 2 DC in each stitch, chain 2, turn (16 DC)

Row 3: [2 DC in first stitch, DC in next] (4x), 2 SC, SC in next, *2 DC, DC in next, repeat from * till end, fasten off leaving long tail

Right Ear

Magic Ring, chain 2 and make 8 DC in ring, pull tight but do not join. You should have a half circle, chain 2, turn

Row 2: 2 DC in each stitch, chain 2, turn (16 DC)

Row 3: 2 DC in first stitch, DC in next, repeat till end, chain 2, turn (24 DC)

Row 4: [2 DC in first stitch, DC in next 2] (3x), 2 SC, SC in next 2, *2 DC, DC in next 2, repeat from * until end. Fasten off leaving long tail.

Inside Right Ear

Magic Ring, chain 2 and make 8 DC in ring, pull tight but do not join. You should have a half circle, chain 2, turn

Row 2: 2 DC in each stitch, chain 2, turn (16 DC)

Row 3: [2 DC in first stitch, DC in next] (3x), 2 SC, SC in next, *2 DC, DC in next, repeat from * till end, fasten off leaving long tail

Trunk

Magic Ring, chain 1 and make 10 SC in ring, join, continue to SC in rounds

Round 2: in back loops only, SC in each stitch around (10 SC)

Rounds 3-5: SC in each stitch around

Round 6: SC decrease, 2 SC, SC in next 3 stitches, 2 SC, SC in next 3 stitches

Round 7: SC decrease, SC in next 9 stitches

Round 8: SC decrease, 2 SC, SC in next 3 stitches, 2 SC, SC in next 3 stitches

Round 9: 2 SC in first, SC in next 4, 2 SC, SC in next 4 stitches

Round 10: SC in each stitch around (12 SC)

Round 11: 2 SC, SC in next 3 stitches, repeat around (15 SC)

Round 12: SC in each stitch around (15 SC)

Fasten off leaving long tail.

Stuff trunk lightly and sew onto middle-front of hat.

Sew inside ears to outer ears and sew onto sides of hat.

Sew two black buttons on for eyes, right above trunk.

Colorful Hat for Newborn Boy

Materials

Yarn: Martha Stewart Crafts from Lion Brand Yarn – Extra Soft Wool Blend in Sailor Blue, Holly Berry, Winter Sky, Buttermilk, Green Eucalyptus

Hook: H, 5 mm

Tapestry needle to sew in tails

Abbreviations

CH = chain

HDC = half double crochet

ST = stitch

SL ST = slip stitch

Pattern for Preemies (13 to 14 inch head)

The Crown

CH 3, SL ST to form a ring

Round 1:

CH 2 (counts as first HDC), 11 HDC in ring (12 HDC total)

SL ST to top of CH 2

Round 2

CH 2 (counts as first HDC), 1 HDC in same space

2 HDC in each space around (24 HDC total)

SL ST to top of CH 2

Round 3

CH 2 (counts as first HDC)

1 HDC in each space (24 total)

SL ST to top of CH 2

Round 4

CH 2 (counts as first HDC), 1 HDC in same space

1 HDC in next space

*2 HDC in next space

1 HDC in next space*

Repeat from * all the way around (36 HDC total)

SL ST to top of CH 2

The Side of the Hat

Rounds 5-15

CH 2 (counts as first HDC),

1 HDC in each space (36 HDC total)

SL ST to top of CH 2

Cuff – Work 5 or 6 rows for a cuff, using white and red yarn, but work on the inside of the hat so when the cuff is turned up, that will be the right side of your work.

Color Changes

Round 6 – red (holly berry)

Round 7 – white (buttermilk)

Round 8: dark blue (sailor blue)

Round 9: green (green eucalyptus)

Round 10: red (holly berry)

Rounds 11-15 – back to blue (winter sky)

Rounds 15-19 – white (buttermilk)

Round 20: red (holly berry)

Pattern for Newborns (13-15 inch head)

The Crown

CH 3, SL ST to form a ring

Round 1:

CH 2 (counts as first HDC), 11 HDC in ring (12 HDC total)

SL ST to top of CH 2

Round 2

CH 2 (counts as first HDC), 1 HDC in same space

2 HDC in each space around (24 HDC total)

SL ST to top of CH 2

Round 3

CH 2 (counts as first HDC), 1 HDC in same space

1 HDC in each of the next 2 spaces

*2 HDC in the next space

1 HDC in each of the next 2 spaces (32 total)

SL ST to top of CH 2

Round 4

CH 2 (counts as first HDC)

1 HDC in each space around (32 total)

SL ST to top of CH 2

Round 5

CH 2 (counts as first HDC), 1 HDC in same space

1 HDC in each of the next 3 spaces

*2 HDC in the next space

1 HDC in each of the next 3 spaces*

Repeat from * all the way around (40 HDC total)

SL ST to top of CH 2

The Side of the Hat

If you want this hat to be bigger, use my hat measurement guide to determine the size of the crown you need, then continue to add increasing rows by adding one or more extra single HDC in between each increasing stitch (which is 2 HDC).

Rounds 6-20

CH 2 (counts as first HDC),

1 HDC in each space (40 HDC total)

SL ST to top of CH 2

Cuff – Work 5 or 6 rows for a cuff, using white and red yarn, but work on the inside of the hat so when the cuff is turned up, that will be the right side of your work.

Color Changes

Round 6 – red (holly berry)

Round 7 – white (buttermilk)

Round 8: dark blue (sailor blue)

Round 9: green (green eucalyptus)

Round 10: red (holly berry)

Rounds 11-20 – back to blue (winter sky)

Rounds 21-24 – white (buttermilk)

Round 25: red (holly berry)

Pink Ruffle Hat

Crochet Hook G/6 or 4 mm hook

Yarn Weight (3) Light/DK (21-24 stitches to 4 inches)

MATERIALS:

- 1 Ball Bernat® Baby Jacquards (100 g /3.5 oz) #06415 (Cherry Berry)

- Crochet Hook: Size 4 mm (U.S. G or 6) crochet hook or size needed to obtain gauge.

GAUGE:

19 sc and 20 rows = 4" [10 cm].

SIZE:

To fit child sizes 6 (12-18-24) mos.

INSTRUCTIONS:

Ch 4. Join with sl st in first ch to form a ring.

1st rnd: Ch 1. 6 sc in ring. Join with sl st in first sc.

2nd rnd: Ch 1. 2 sc in each sc around. Join with sl st in first sc. 12 sc.

3rd rnd: Ch 1. *2 sc in next sc. 1 sc in next sc. Rep from * around. Join with sl st in first sc. 18 sc.

4th rnd: Ch 1. *2 sc in next sc. 1 sc in each of next 2 sc. Rep from * around. Join with sl st in first sc. 24 sc.

5th rnd: Ch 1. *2 sc in next sc. 1 sc in each of next 3 sc. Rep from * around. Join with sl st in first sc. 30 sc.

6th rnd: Ch 1. *2 sc in next sc. 1 sc in each of next 4 sc. Rep from * around. Join with sl st in first sc. 36 sc.

7th rnd: Ch 1. *2 sc in next sc. 1 sc in each of next 5 sc. Rep from * around. Join with sl st in first sc. 42 sc.

8th and alt rnds: Ch 1. 1 sc in each sc around. Join with sl st in first sc.

9th rnd: Ch 1. *2 sc in next sc. 1 sc in each of next 6 sc. Rep from * around. Join with sl st in first sc. 48 sc.

11th rnd: Ch 1. *2 sc in next sc. 1 sc in each of next 7 sc. Rep from * around. Join with sl st in first sc. 54 sc.

12th rnd: As 8th rnd.

Cont in same manner, inc 6 sts on next and every following alt rnd to 72 (78- 84- 90) sc. Place marker at end of last rnd. Rep 8th rnd until work from marked rnd measures 3 (3½-3¾-4) ins [7.5 (9- 9.5-10) cm].

Ruffle: Next rnd: Ch 4 (counts as dc and ch 1). (1 dc. Ch 1. 1 dc) in same sp as sl st. *(Ch 1. 1 dc) 3 times in next sc. Rep from * around. Ch 1. Join with sl st to 3rd ch of ch 4. Fasten off.

Baby Sweaters

BABY SWEATERS

Easy Crochet Baby Cardigan

Item to be need:

Grape color worsted yarn 4ply

Crochet needle

Matching Buttons

Special stitch: (double crochet in first st, slip stitch in next stitch)

Size: Baby size 0-3 months

Gauge 8 hdc x 6 rows = 2 inches

Hook size. 3mm / US D 3.25mm

US Terms

ABBREVIATIONS:

c.	crochet
ch.	Chain
sc	single crochet
hdc	half double crochet
dc.	double crochet
sts.	Stitches
st.	stitch
slst.	Slip stitch
sks.	Skip stitch
FP.	front post
BP.	back post
inc.	increase

Pattern:

Back:

Row 1: To begin ch 53,1dc into the 4th ch from the hook, 1dc into the next ch across. (50+ch 3)

Row 2:   ch3, 1dc FP in next st, 1dc BP into next st, repeat in each st across, at the last st 1dc,

        turn. (50+ch3)

Row 3:   ch1, 1sc in each st across, turn. (50+ch1)

Row 4-19: ch1, 1hdc in each st across, turn. (50+ch1)

Make the arm shape:

Row 20: ch1, slst into the top of the 3sts, hdc into the next sts, leave the last 4sts un worked,

        ch1 turn. (42hdc)

Row 21-32: ch1, 1hdc in each st across, (42 hdc)

Fasten off.

Right front:

Row 1: To begin ch 25,1dc into the 4th ch from the hook, 1dc into the next ch across. (22+ch3)

Row 2:   ch3, 1dc FP in next st, 1dc BP into next st, repeat in each st across, at the last st

1dc, turn. (22+ch3)

Row 3:   ch1, 1sc in each st across, turn. (22+ch1)

Row 4-7: ch1, 1hdc in each st across, turn. (22+ch1)

Pattern row:

Row 8:   ch1, slst into the base of the ch1, 1dc in next st, slst in next st, repeat (dc, slst)

across, turn.(22sts)

Row 9:   ch1, 1hdc in each st across, turn. (22+ch1)

Row 10-21:   repeat (Row 8, Row 9)

Make the arm shape:

Row 22:   ch1, slst into the top of the 3sts, 1hdc into the next sts acraoss, turn.(19sts)

Row 23-26:   ch1, 1hdc in each st across (19sts)

Make the neck shape:

Row 27:   ch1, slst in next 2sts, 1hdc into the next sts across, ch1 turn.(17sts)

Row 28:   ch1, 1hdc in each st across (17sts)

Row 29:   ch1, slst in next 2sts, 1hdc into the next sts across, ch1 turn. (15sts)

Row 30-34:   ch1. 1hdc in each st across (15sts)

30

Fasten off.

Left front:

Row 1- 21: follow the right front pattern.(22)

Make the arm shape:

Row 22: ch1, 1hdc into next sts, leave the last 3sts, un worked, ch1 turn. (19sts)

Row23-26: ch1, 1hdc in each st across, ch1, turn. (19)

Make the neck shape:

Row27: ch1,1hdc in each st across, leave 2 sts un worked, ch1, turn. (17)

Row28: ch1,1hdc in each st across, ch1, turn. (17)

Row29: ch1,1hdc in each st across, leave 2 sts un worked, ch1, turn. (15)

Row 30-34: ch1, 1hdc in each st across (15sts)

Fasten off.

Make sleeves x 2:

Row 1: To begin ch 33, 1dc into the 4th ch from the hook, 1dc into the next ch across. (30+ch3)

Row 2: ch3, 1dc FP in next st, 1dc BP into next st, repeat in each st across, at the last st 1dc,

   turn. (30+ch3)

Row 3: ch1, 1sc in each st across, turn. (30+ch1)

Row 4-5: ch1, 1hdc in each st across, turn. (30+ch1)

Pattern row:

Row 6:   ch1, slst into the base of the ch1, 1dc in next st, slst in next st, repeat (dc, slst) across,

          turn. (30sts)

Row 7:   ch1, 1hdc in each st across, (30+ch1)

Row 8:   repeat (Row6) (30+ch1)

Row 9:   repeat (Row7) (30+ch1)

Row 10:   repeat (Row6) (30+ch1)

Row 11:   INC, ch1, 2hdc into 1st st, 1hdc into next sts, at the last st , (INC)2hdc, turn.(32+ch1)

Row 12:   repeat (Row6) (32+ch1)

Row 13:   INC   repeat (Row11) (34+ch1)

Row 14:   repeat (Row7) (34+ch1)

Row 15:   INC   repeat (Row11) (36+ch1)

Row 16:   repeat (Row7) (36+ch1)

Row 17:   INC   repeat (Row11) (38+ch1)

Row 18:   repeat (Row7) (38+ch1)

Row 19:   INC   repeat (Row11) (40+ch1)

Row 20:   repeat (Row7) (40+ch1)

Row 21:   INC   repeat (Row11) (42+ch1)

33

Row 22:   repeat (Row7) (42+ch1)

Fasten off.

Make the right and left button band:

Work: with the right side facing join the yarn with a slst into the corner, starting with ch3,

Work 26 dc evenly along front edge to neck corner, turn. (26dc)

Next round: ch3, 1dc FP in next st, 1dc BP into next st, repeat in each st along the band.

work same in both of the band.Fasten off

Sewing:

With the wrong side of the back part and left, right front parts together sew the shoulders

seems together with a crochet needle or slst with a crochet hook. then make the neck band.

 And then join the sleeves to the jacket in both of the sides.

Make the neck band:

With the right side facing join the yarn to neck edge after right front band, starting with ch3, work 52 dc evenly around neck edge to before front band on the second left band, turn.(52dc)

Next round: ch3, 1dc FP in next st, 1dc BP into next st, repeat in each st along the neck band.

Fasten off.

Finishing: sew the matching buttons on the right side of the jacket.

Hat Pattern:

Hat Pattern:

Make a magic ring.

Rnd1: (ch1 as count) 11hdc into the magic ring, slst, turn (12hdc)

Rnd2: (ch1 as count) 1hdc into the same st, 2hdc into the next sts, repeat, slst, turn. (24hdc)

Rnd3: (ch1 as count) 2hdc into the next st, repeat (1hdc, 2hdc) around, slst, turn. (36hdc)

Hat Pattern:

35

repeat (1hdc into 2sts, 2hdc in next) around, slst, turn. (48hdc)

Rnd5-7: (ch1 as count) 1hdc in each st around, slst, turn.(48hdc)

Pattern row:

Rnd8: ch1, slst into the base of the ch1, 1dc in next st, slst in next st, repeat (dc, slst) around, slst, turn.(48)

Rnd 9: ch1, 1hdc in each st around, slst, turn. (48)

Rnd 10: repeat (Rnd8) (48)

Rnd11-13: repeat (Rnd9) (48)

Rnd 14: ch3, 1dc in each st around.slst. (48)

Rnd 15: ch3, 1dc FP in next st, 1dc BP into next st, repeat in each st around, Slst to join. Fasten off.

Abigail Baby Girl Cardigan

YARN

275 yards of thin worsted weight yarn in main color and small amount for border, I used Carons Simply Soft in soft pink and soft heather grey, other worsted weight yarns may produce different results, please check your gauge

MATERIALS

5.5mm (I) hook

Yarn needle

DIFFICULTY

Easy

FINISHED SIZE

10" at longest height

9 1/2" at widest part across chest

9" from top of should to end of sleeves

This sweater should comfortably fit a baby 6-12 months old.

GAUGE

13 sts and 7 rows = 4" x 4"

STITCH GUIDE

mc – main color, bc – border color, ch(s) – chain(s), sc – single crochet, hdc – half double crochet, dc – double crochet, st(s) – stitch(es), RS – right side,

SPECIAL STITCHES

39

dc3tog- double crochet three together

YO, insert hook in first st, YO, pull up loop, draw through first two loops on hook (two loops remaining on hook), *YO insert hook in next st, YO, pull up loop, draw through first two loops on hook** (three loops remaining on hook). Repeat from * to ** (four loops remaining on hook). YO and draw through all four loops on hook.

dc2tog– double crochet two together

yarn over (YO), insert hook into first st, YO and draw up a loop, (three loops on hook), YO and pull through first two loops (two loops remaining on hook), YO, insert hook in next st, YO and draw up a loop (four loops on hook), YO, pull through first two loops on hook, YO and pull through remaining three loops.

NOTES

- Ch 3 is considered the first dc. The next dc will be placed in the 2nd st from hook

- Ch 1 is NOT considered the first st

- Body of sweater is worked in rows, raglan style
- Sleeves are stitched into body in rounds

PATTERN

YOKE

Row 1: Ch 45, turn, 1sc in each st across. <44>

Row 2: Ch 3, dc in each of the next 2sts, 2 dc in the next st, *dc in each of the next 3sts, 2 dc in the next st, repeat from * to end <55>

Row 3: Ch 3, dc in each of the next 3sts, 2 dc in the next st, *dc in each of the next 4sts, 2 dc in the next st, repeat from * to end <66>

Row 4: Ch 3, dc in each of the next 4sts, 2 dc in the next st, *1dc in each of the next 5sts, 2 dc in the next st, repeat from * to end <77>

Row 5: Ch 3, dc in each of the next 5sts, 2 dc in the next st, *1dc in each of the next 6sts, 2 dc in the next st, repeat from * to end <88>

Row 6: Ch 3, dc in each of the next 6sts, 2 dc in the next st, *1dc in each of the next 7sts, 2 dc in the next st, repeat from * to end <99>

Row 7: Ch 3, dc in each of the next 7sts, 2 dc in the next st, *dc in each of the next 8sts, 2 dc in the next st, repeat from * to end <110>

SEPARATE FOR SLEEVES

Row 8: Ch 3, dc in each of the next 14sts, ch 3 and skip 24sts, dc in each of the next 32sts, ch 3 and skip 24sts, dc in each of the next 15sts

the next 3sts, 2 dc in the next st, repeat from * to end <55>

41

Rows 10 – 19: Ch 3, dc in each of the next 67 sts, on last st change to border color. <68>

Row 20: Ch 1 and sc in same st, sc in each st <68>

Row 21: Ch 1 and sc in same st, sc in each st <68>

EDGING

I like the design feature of the gaps where the edging meets the body, if you do not want gaps in your edging, place your sts in the ch 3/dc at the ends of rows as opposed to the spaces made by the ch 3/dc as written in pattern.

Working up the front of the sweater, 2 sc in each ch3 space (16 spaces), sc in the top row and continue to sc around the entire neck. Working back down the front, sc in the top row, 2 sc in each of the ch3 spaces (16 spaces) and fasten off at bottom. Fasten off and weave in ends

SLEEVES

43

Round 1: Attach yarn with sl st under arm, in st before the three underarm ch sts, ch 3, dc3tog in the 3 underarm ch sts, dc in each of the next 27sts <29>

Round 2: Ch 3, dc2tog, dc in each of the next 26 sts <28>

Round 3: Ch 3, dc2tog, dc in each of the next 25sts <27>

Round 4: Ch 3, dc2tog, dc in each of the next 24 sts <26>

Round 5: Ch 3, dc2tog, dc in each of the next 23 sts <25>

Rounds 6-12: Ch 3, dc in every st around <25>

Round 13: Change to border color. Ch 1, sc in the same st and in every st around, sl st into first sc to join.

Repeat for other sleeve

FINISHING

Fasten off and weave in all ends

Crochet Granny Square Baby Sweater

Materials You will need for your Granny Square sweater:

Baby weight 3 (fine) yarn in colors of your choice.. it takes less than 3 oz of each color.

Scissors

Scissors

Yarn needle

45

G Crochet Hook (4mm)

1 yard of a soft coordinating ribbon (optional) you can choose to just chain 50 and use that as your tie

To begin: Make 12 granny squares

Granny square pattern: (I used 2 colors, you can change colors each round if you like)   Are you ready? "Let's Get The Party Started!"

Instructions:
(color 1)   chain 4, sl st into 1st ch

rnd 1: ch 3 (counts as dc here and thru out), 2dc into ring, *ch 3, 3dc into ring*, rep from * to * 2 more times, sl st into 3rd ch, sl into next 2 st, sl st into ch-3 space (you will be working inside the corner space)

rnd 2: ch 3, 2dc into ch-3 sp, ch 3, *3dc into ch-3 sp, ch 2, 3dc into ch-3 sp,*, rep from * to * two more times.sl st into 3rd ch, sl into next 2 st, sl into ch-3

46

space. **Change color** before completing your sl st in the ch-3 sp (you will be working inside the corner space)

46

rnd 3: (with color 2) ch 3, 2dc into ch-3 sp, ch 3, *3dc into ch-3 sp, ch 2, 3dc into ch-3 sp,*, rep from * to * two more times,sl st into 3rd ch, sl into next 2 st, sl into ch-3 space.

rnd 4:ch 3, 2dc into ch-3 sp, ch 3, *3dc into ch-3 sp, ch 2, 3dc into ch-3 sp,*, rep from * to * two more times,sl st into 3rd ch, sl into next 2 st, sl into ch-3 space. fasten off.

Check "Putting all together" section for further instructions.

Putting it all together:

After completing your 12 granny squares, you will be making 6 pieces of two squares each. This will give your 6 pieces that have 2 squares each (these 2 pieces will be forming a rectangle) These 6 pieces is what you will be using to shape your sweater.   Begin your seam on the 2nd ch of each corner and end on the following 2nd ch of the of that edge. Line up your squares to ensure you are sewing them correctly. Do this with all your pieces. Please NOTE: Be sure your are sewing the same sides together, meaning both right sides should be facing in

space. **Change color** before completing your sl st in the ch-3 sp (you will be working inside the corner space)

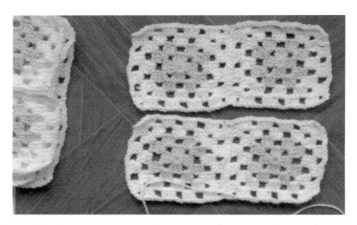

If you're not sure how to sew your seams together or you need a reminder I have a quick video tutorial. Just click on the link or picture below.

Back of **Granny square sweater**: Take 2 of your rectangles and sew them together along one edge to form a square. There will be four granny squares in this piece. (see photo)

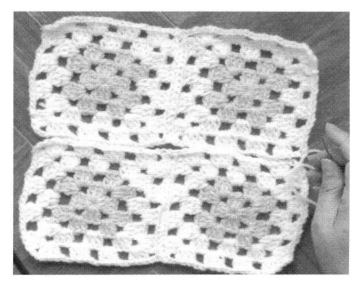

Front of **Granny square sweater**: Now you will be sewing the front pieces to your sweater. You will begin at the outer corner (the 2nd chain) and this time you will sew across and stop after the third double crochet of the second 3dc cluster. You will leave the remaining stitches free. This will form the neck opening. See photo below. Do this on both edges. Always ensure that the right

opening. See photo below. Do this on both edges. Always ensure that the right side of the work is facing you).

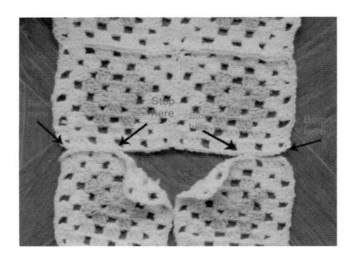

Sleeves of **Granny square sweater:** Now take the remaining 2 pieces and line them up along the 2 squares in the center. Meaning the back of sweater and the front of the sweater. Sew your pieces the same way. Beginning on the first side 2nd chain and ending on the 2nd chain of your edge. Your piece should resemble

side of the work is facing you).

Sewing up sleeve and side seams: Now fold your piece with the back to the back and front to the front. You will be folding your sleeves to have one square to the back and one to the front. Sew along the side seams to close your sweater. See photo.

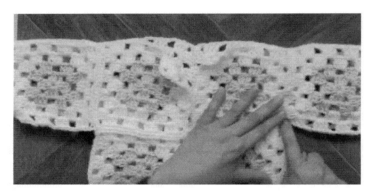

Finishing edge: Join yarn (your choice of color) along a stitch in the back of the sweater. Now, chain 1, and work 3 rows of single crochet around edges in front, back, and neck. **Work 3 single crochet on the corner stitches of each row**. Do the same for the sleeves. Fasten off.
Sew in all your tails.

Take your ribbon and feed it thru the front. I usually go to the second chain -3 space to avoid having it too close to the neck. You are ready to enjoy your sweater.

Frutti Toddler Poncho

Crochet Hook H/8 or 5 mm hook

Yarn Weight (4) Medium Weight/Worsted Weight and Aran (16-20 stitches to 4 inches)

SIZES

12–24 months, (2–4 years)

FINISHED MEASUREMENTS

Neck Circumference: 17 (19)"/43 (48.5)cm

Length: 10 (12)"/25.5 (30.5)cm

MATERIALS:

- Stitch.Rock.Love. Sheep(ish) from Caron (70% Acrylic/30% Wool; 3oz/85g, 167yds/153m):
    - 0018 Robin Egg(ish) (A): 1 ball
    - 0021 Lime(ish) (B): 1 ball

- o 0014 Coral(ish) (C): 1 ball
- o 0004 White(ish) (D): 1 ball
- One size US H-8 (5mm) crochet hook, or size to obtain gauge.
- Stitch markers
- 3" piece of heavy cardboard (or pompom maker)

- Yarn needle

GAUGE

In pattern stitch, 14 sts and 8 rows = 4"/10cm.

STITCHES USED

Chain (ch), double crochet (dc), half double crochet (hdc), single crochet (sc), slip stitch (sl st)

NOTE

Poncho is worked in joined rounds, with right side facing at all times. Join with a sl st at the end of each round, but do not turn.

PONCHO

Cowl

With A, ch 60 (66), taking care not to twist ch, join with sl st in first ch to form a ring

Round 1 (RS): Ch 3 (counts as first dc), dc in each remaining ch around; join with sl st in top of beginning ch—60 (66) sts. Do not fasten off A. Carry color not in use up inside of piece until next needed.

56

Round 2 (RS): Draw up a loop of B in same ch as join; with B, ch 2, hdc in each st around; join with sl st in top of beginning ch. Do not fasten off B. Carry color not in use up inside of piece until next needed.

Round 3 (RS): Draw up a loop of A in same ch as join; with A, ch 3, dc in each st around; join with sl st in top of beginning ch.

Rounds 4–7: Repeat Rounds 2 and 3 twice.

Fasten off A and B.

Body

Lay cowl flat to find sides. Place one marker on each side, one on left and one on right side with equal amount of space between them on front and back.

Round 8 (RS): Draw up a loop of C in same ch as join; with C, ch 3, dc in each st to first marker, 2 dc in marked st, move marker to last dc made, dc in each st to next marker, 2 dc in marked st, move marker to last dc made, dc in each st to end of round; join with sl st in top of beginning ch—62 (68) sts. Move markers up as each round is completed.

Rounds 9–10 (11): Ch 3, [dc in each st to next marker, 2 dc in marked st] twice, dc in each st to end of round; join with sl st in top of beginning ch—66 (74) sts. Fasten off C.

57

Round 11 (12): Draw up a loop of B in same ch as join; with B, ch 2, [hdc in each st to next marker, 2 hdc in marked st] twice, hdc in each st to end of round; join with sl st in top of beginning ch—68 (76) sts. Fasten off B.

Rounds 12 (13): Draw up a loop of A in same ch as join; with A, ch 3, [dc in each st to next marker, 2 dc in marked st] twice, dc in each st to end of round; join with sl st in top of beginning ch—70 (78) sts.

Rounds 13 (14)–14 (16): With A, repeat Round 9—74 (84) sts. Fasten off A.

Round 15 (17): Repeat Round 11 (12)—76 (86) sts. Fasten off B.

Rounds 16 (18): Repeat Round 8—78 (88) sts.

Rounds 17 (19)–19 (23): Ch 3, [dc in each st to next marker, 2 dc in marked st] twice, dc in each st to end of round; join with sl st in top of beginning ch—84 (96) sts. Fasten off C.

Picot Edging (RS): Draw up a loop of D in same ch as join, *ch 4, sl st in 3rd ch from hook (picot made); repeat from * around. Fasten off.

TIE

With D, make a chain that measures about 43"/109cm, leaving long beginning and ending tails for tying pompoms to end of tie.

FINISHING

Weave tie in and out of base of cowl (Round 7), beginning and ending at front of poncho.

Pompoms (make 2)

Using D and 3"/7.5cm piece of cardboard, wrap yarn around cardboard about 30 times. Slip wraps off cardboard and tie a piece of yarn tightly around the center of the wraps. Cut both ends of wraps and fluff pompom. Trim.

Using beginning and ending tails of tie, tie one pompom to each end. Using yarn needle, weave in all ends.

Banana Split Baby Vest

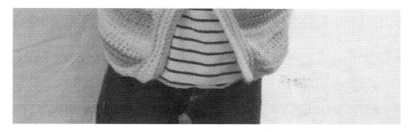

rochet HookG/6 or 4 mm hook

Yarn Weight(2) Fine (23-26 stitches to 4 inches)
MATERIALS:

- Lion Brand Yarn, 923-204 Ice Cream, 1 ball
- Lion Brand Crochet Hook: G/6 (4 mm)
- Split Ring Stitch Markers
- Large-Eye Blunt Needles
- 3 Buttons, about 1/2 in. (13 mm) diameter
- Sewing Needle and Thread

SIZE:

Child (Multiple Sizes)

6-9 months (12-18 months, 2 year)

Finished Chest: About 18 1/2 (20 1/2, 21 1/2) in. (47 (52, 54.5) cm), buttoned.

Finished Length: About 11 1/2 (12 1/4, 13) in. (29 (31, 33) cm)

GAUGE:

15 hdc + 13 rows = about 4 in. (10 cm).

STITCH:

hdc2tog: (hdc 2 sts together) (Yarn over, insert hook in next st and draw up a loop) twice, yarn over and draw through all 5 loops on hook – 1 st decreased.

NOTES:

1. Vest is worked in one piece beginning at lower edge, then divided for armholes.

2. End with a WS row means that the last row you work should be a WS row, and the next row that you are ready to work will be a RS row.

3. When you see '– 12 sts' in the instructions, this lets you know how many sts you will have at the end of that specific row.

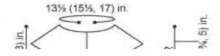

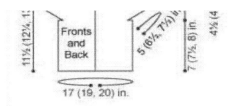

VEST

Ch 64 (72, 76).

Row 1 (RS): Sc in 2nd ch from hook and in each ch across — 63 (71, 75) sc.

Rows 2-6: Ch 1, turn, working in back loops only, sc in each st across.

Row 7: Ch 2 (beg ch counts as first hdc), turn, hdc in next st and in each st across — 63 (71, 75) hdc.

Rep Row 7 until piece measures about 7 (7 1/2, 8) in. (18 (19, 20.5) cm) from beg, end with a WS row as the last row you work.

Next Row (RS): Ch 1, turn, working in back loops only, sc in each st across.

Rep last row once more.

Divide for Armholes

Row 1 (RS): Ch 1, turn, working in back loops only, sc in first 13 (14, 15) sc, ch 20 (24, 28), sk next 4 (6, 6) sc, sc in next 29 (31, 33) sc, ch 20 (24, 28), sk next 4 (6, 6) sc, sc in next 13 (14, 15) sc —55 (59, 63) sc and 2 ch-20 (24, 28) loops.

Row 2: Ch 1, turn, working in back loops only, sc in first 13 (14,15) sc, place marker (pm), sc in next 20 (24, 28) ch, pm, sc in next 29 (31, 33) sc, pm, sc in next 20 (24, 28) ch, pm, sc in next 13 (14,15) sc – 95 (107, 119) sc.

Note: Move markers up as you complete each row.

Rows 3-5: Ch 1, turn, working in back loops only, sc in each st across.

63

Row 6: Ch 2 (counts as first hdc), turn, hdc in next st, (hdc in each st to 2 sts before marker, hdc2tog, move marker to hdc2tog just made, hdc2tog) 4 times, hdc in each st to end of row – 87 (99, 111) hdc rem.

Rows 7-10 (11, 12): Rep Row 6 – 55 (59, 63) hdc rem on last row worked.

Row 11 (12, 13): Ch 1, turn, working in back loops only, sc in each st to end of row.

Rep last row 5 more times.

Fasten off.

FINISHING

Buttonband

From RS, join yarn with a sl st at neck edge of left front for girl's vest or at lower corner of right front for boy's vest.

Row 1 (RS): Ch 1, work 34 (38, 42) sc evenly spaced along front edge.

Rows 2-8: Ch 1, turn, working in back loops only, sc in each st across. Fasten off.

Place 3 markers along buttonband for buttons as follows: 1/2 in. (1.5 cm), 2 1/2 in. (6.5 cm) and 4 1/2 in. (11.5 cm) down from neck edge.

Buttonhole Band

From RS, join yarn with a sl st at lower corner of right front for girl's vest or neck edge of left front for boy's vest.

Row 1 (RS): Ch 1, work 34 (38, 42) sc evenly spaced along front edge.

Rows 2-4: Ch 1, turn, working in back loops only, sc in each st across.

Row 5: Ch 1, turn, working in back loops only, sc in each st across, working (ch 1, sk next st) opposite each button marker.

Rows 6-8: Ch 1, turn, working in back loops only, sc in each st and ch-1 sp across.

Fasten off.

With sewing needle and thread, sew buttons to Buttonband opposite buttonholes. Weave in ends.

BOOTIES

Sleepy Panda Baby Booties

MATERIALS

3.5mm (E/4) Crochet Hook

85yds [100yds] DK (8ply) Yarn – Drops Cotton Light (115yds/50g)

– "Black/20" (1 [1] skeins)

– "White/02" (1 [1] skeins)

Tapestry Needle

FINISHED SIZE

Pattern is made for 0 – 6 months old. Changes for size 6- 12 months are in [ ].

Finished Measurements (Sole Length)

0 – 6 Months: 3.5" (9cm)

6 – 12 Months: 4" (10cm)

GAUGE

20 stitches + 16 rows = 4"/10cm in half double crochet

STITCHES & ABBREVIATIONS

st(s) – stitch(es)

ch – chain stitch

sl st – slip stitch

sc – single crochet

hdc – half double crochet

sc2tog – single crochet 2 together

hdc2tog – half double crochet 2 together

Single Crochet 2 Together (sc2tog)

Insert your hook into the next stitch. Yarn over, pull back through that stitch (2 loops on hook). Insert your hook into the next stitch. Yarn over, pull back through that stitch (3 loops on hook). Yarn over, pull through all the loops on your hook.

Half Double Crochet 2 Together (hdc2tog)

Yarn over, insert hook into next stitch. Yarn over, pull back through stitch (3 loops on hook). Yarn over, Insert hook into next stitch. Yarn over, pull back through stitch (5 loops on hook). Yarn over pull through all the loops on your hook.

SKILL LEVEL

This is an "Easy" level crochet pattern (includes "How-To" photos). You must be familiar with basic crochet stitches and techniques. Directions written so that they are easy to read and follow. All patterns are in English, and written in standard US terms.

+ **PATTERN**

Note: The 'Sole' of this bootie is worked in the round. The 'Top' of this bootie is worked in the round, from bottom to top.

+ **SOLE**

Ch11 [13] using 'Black' yarn and 3.5mm hook.

Rnd 1: 2 hdc in 2nd ch from hook, 1 hdc in next 8 [10] sts, 5 hdc in next st. (Note: You are now going to be working on the opposite side of foundation chain.) 1 hdc in next 8 [10] sts. 3 hdc in last st. (26 [30] sts) Do not sl st in 1 st hdc of this rnd.

Rnd 2: Start crocheting in 1st st from the previous rnd. 2 hdc in next 2 sts. 1 hdc in next 8 [10] sts. 2 hdc in next 5 sts. 1 hdc in next 8 [10] sts. 2 hdc in next 3 sts.

(36 [40] sts) Do not sl st in 1st hdc of this rnd.

Rnd 3: Start crocheting in 1st st from the previous rnd. *2 hdc in next st. 1 hdc in next st. Repeat from the * twice. 1 hdc in next 8 [10] sts. *2 hdc in next st. 1 hdc in next st. Repeat from the * 5 times. 1 hdc in next 8 [10] sts. *2 hdc in next st. 1

hdc in next st. Repeat from the * 3 times. Sl st in 1st st of this rnd. (46 [50] sts) Fasten off, and weave in loose ends.

+ TOP OF SHOE

Rnd 1: Attach yarn (Black) right in the middle of the heel. Ch1, 1 sc in the same st, but only through the back loop. (Note: Continue crocheting the sts in this rnd, only in the back loop.) 1 sc in next 45 [49] sts. Do not sl st in 1st sc of this rnd.

70

Rnd 2 — 3: Start crocheting in 1st st from the previous rnd. 1 sc in every st all around. Do not sl st in 1st sc of this rnd. (Note: If you're creating the 6 — 12 month size, add 1 extra rnd to the original 2.)

Rnd 4: Start crocheting in 1st st from the previous rnd. 1 sc in next 13 [15] sts. *1 sc2tog. 1 sc in next st. Repeat from the * 7 times. 1 sc in next 12 [14] sts. Do not sl st in 1st sc of this rnd. (39 [43] sts)

Rnd 5: Start crocheting in 1st st from the previous rnd. 1 sc in 1st st, 1 sc2tog. 1 sc in next 9 [11] sts. *1 sc2tog. 1 sc in next st. Repeat from the * 5 times. 1 sc in next 9 [11] sts. 1 sc2tog. 1 sc in next st. Do not sl st in 1st sc of this rnd. (32 [36] sts)

Rnd 6: Start crocheting in 1st st from the previous rnd. 1 sc in next 15 [17] sts. 2 hdc2tog. 1 sc in next 13 [15] sts. Do not sl st in 1st sc of this rnd. (30 [34] sts)

hdc2tog. 1 sc in next 15 [15] sts. Do not sl st in 1st sc of this rnd. (30 [34] sts)

Rnd 7: Start crocheting in 1st st from the previous rnd. 1 sc in next 30 [34] Sl st in 1st st of this rnd.

Fasten off, and weave in loose ends.

+ HEAD

Rnd 1: Ch2 using "White" yarn, 6 hdc in 2nd ch from hook, Join with sl st in first hdc. (6 sts)

Rnd 2: Ch1. 2 hdc in next 6 sts. Join with sl st in first hdc. (12 sts)

71

Rnd 3: Ch1, 1 hdc in same st. 2 hdc in next 4 sts. 1 hdc in next 2 sts. 2 hdc in next 4 sts. 1 hdc in next st. Join with sl st in first hdc. (20 sts)

Rnd 4: Ch1, 1 sc in same st. 1 sc in next st. 2 sc in next 6 sts. 1 sc in next 4 sts. 2 sc in next 6 sts. 1 sc in next 2 sts. Join with sl st in first sc. (32 sts)

Fasten off, and weave in loose ends.

Repeat "Head" pattern four times. Sew/join 2 together, making sure to stuff the head with a bit of toy stuffing before completely sewing the 2 sections together.

Sew a completed "Head" onto each bootie, towards the front. Embroider a pair of sleepy eyes onto each head using black yarn.

+ EARS & NOSE

Ears

Rnd 1: Ch2 using "Black" yarn, 4 hdc in 2nd ch from hook. Ch2. Join with sl st in first hdc. (4 sts)

Fasten off, and weave in loose ends.

Repeat "Ear" pattern four times. Sew 2 ears onto each head, towards the top, making sure to space them out evenly.

Nose

Using black yarn, Ch3, then sl st in first ch.

Fasten off, and weave in loose ends.

Repeat "Nose" pattern twice. Sew 1 nose onto each head, just beneath the sleepy eyes.

Ellie The Elephant Crochet Baby Booties

MATERIALS

3.5mm (E/4) Crochet Hook

95yds [120yds] Drops Muskat (109yds/50g) – "Light Blue Purple" (1 [2] skeins)

Tapestry Needle

FINISHED SIZE

Pattern is made for 0 – 6 months old. Changes for size 6- 12 months are in [ ].

Finished Measurements (Sole Length)

0 – 6 Months: 3.5" (9cm)

6 – 12 Months: 4" (10cm)

GAUGE

20 stitches + 16 rows = 4"/10cm in half double crochet

STITCHES & ABBREVIATIONS

st(s) – stitch(es)

ch – chain stitch

sl st – slip stitch

sc – single crochet

hdc – half double crochet

dc – double crochet

sc2tog – single crochet 2 together

hdc2tog – half double crochet 2 together

dc2tog – double crochet 2 together

camel sc – camel single crochet

Single Crochet 2 Together (sc2tog)

Insert your hook into the next stitch. Yarn over, pull back through that stitch (2 loops on hook). Insert your hook into the next stitch. Yarn over, pull back through that stitch (3 loops on hook). Yarn over, pull through all the loops on your hook.

Camel Single Crochet (camel sc)

Insert your hook into the next stitch, but not through the front OR back loop, but instead an extra loop that is behind the stitch. Yarn over, and pull back through that stitch (2 loops on hook). Yarn over, and pull through all the loops on your hook.

SKILL LEVEL

This is an "Easy" level crochet pattern (includes "How To" photos). You must be

This is an "Easy" level crochet pattern (includes "How-To" photos). You must be familiar with basic crochet stitches and techniques. Directions written so that they are easy to read and follow. All patterns are in English, and written in standard US terms.

+ **PATTERN**

Note: This bootie is worked in the round, from bottom to top. The cuf is worked from the inside of your work/bootie, and in the round.

+ SOLE

Ch11 [13] using yarn and 3.50mm hook.

Rnd 1: 2 hdc in 2nd ch from hook, 1 hdc in next 8 [10] sts, 5 hdc in next st. (Note: You are now going to be working on the opposite side of foundation chain.) 1 hdc in next 8 [10] sts. 3 hdc in last st. (26 [30] sts) Do not sl st in 1st hdc of this rnd.

Rnd 2: Start crocheting in 1st st from the previous rnd. 2 hdc in next 2 sts. 1 hdc in next 8 [10] sts. 2 hdc in next 5 sts. 1 hdc in next 8 [10] sts. 2 hdc in next 3 sts. (36 [40] sts) Do not sl st in 1st hdc of this rnd.

Rnd 3: Start crocheting in 1st st from the previous rnd. *2 hdc in next st. 1 hdc in next st. Repeat from the * twice. 1 hdc in next 8 [10] sts. *2 hdc in next st. 1 hdc in next st. Repeat from the * 5 times. 1 hdc in next 8 [10] sts. *2 hdc in next st. 1 hdc in next st. Repeat from the * 3 times. Sl st in 1st st of this rnd. (46 [50] sts) Fasten off, and weave in loose ends.

78

79

+ TOP OF SHOE

Rnd 1: Attach yarn right in the middle of the heel. Ch1, 1 sc in the same st, but only through the back loop. (Note: Continue crocheting the sts in this rnd, only in the back loop.) 1 sc in next 45 [49] sts. Do not sl st in 1st sc of this rnd. (46 [50] sts)

79

Rnd 2 – 3 [4]: Start crocheting in 1st st from the previous rnd. 1 sc in every st all around. Do not sl st in 1st sc of this rnd.

Rnd 4 [5]: Start crocheting in 1st st from the previous rnd. 1 sc in next 13 [15] sts. *1 sc2tog. 1 sc in next st. Repeat from the * 7 times. 1 sc in next 12 [14] sts. Do not sl st in 1st sc of this rnd. (39 [43] sts)

Rnd 5 [6]: Start crocheting in 1st st from the previous rnd. 1 sc in next st. 1 sc2otg. 1 sc in next 9 [11] sts. *1 sc2tog. 1 sc in next st. Repeat from the * 5 times. 1 sc in next 9 [11] sts. 1 sc2tog. 1 sc in next st. Do not sl st in 1st sc of this rnd. (32 [36] sts)

Rnd 6 [7]: Start crocheting in 1st st from the previous rnd. 1 sc in next 12 [14] sts.

1 hdc2tog, 2 dc2tog, 1 hdc2tog. 1 sc in next 12 [14] sts. Do not sl st in 1st sc of this rnd. (28 [32] sts)

Rnd 7 [8]: Start crocheting in 1st st from the previous rnd. 1 sc in next 13 [15] sts. 2 hdc2tog, 1 sc in next 11 [13] sts. Do not sl st in 1st sc of this rnd. (26 [30] sts)

Rnd 8 [9] – 10 [11]: Start crocheting in 1st st from the previous rnd. 1 sc in every st all around. Do not sl st in 1st sc of this rnd. (26 [30] sts)

Rnd 11 [12]: Start crocheting in 1st st from the previous rnd. 1 camel sc in every st all around. Sl st in 1st st of this rnd. (26 [30] sts)

Fasten off, and weave in loose ends.

+ HEAD

Ch2 using yarn and 3.50mm hook.

Rnd 1: 6 sc in 2nd ch from hook. (6 sts) Do not sl st in 1st sc of this rnd.

Rnd 2: Start crocheting in 1st st from the previous rnd. 2 sc in every st all around. (12 sts) Do not sl st in 1st sc of this rnd.

Rnd 3: Start crocheting in 1st st from the previous rnd. *1 sc in next st, 2 sc in next st. Repeat from the * all around. (18 sts) Do not sl st in 1st sc of this rnd.

Rnd 4: Start crocheting in 1st st from the previous rnd. *1 sc in next 2 sts, 2 sc in next st. Repeat from the * all around. (24 sts) Do not sl st in 1st sc of this rnd.

81

Rnd 5 – 8: Start crocheting in 1st st from the previous rnd. 1 sc in every st all around. (24 sts) Do not sl st in 1st sc of this rnd.

Rnd 9: Start crocheting in 1st st from the previous rnd. *1 sc in next 2 sts, sc2tog. Repeat from the * all around. (18 sts) Do not sl st in 1st sc of this rnd.

Rnd 9: Start crocheting in 1st st from the previous rnd. *1 sc in next st, sc2tog. Repeat from the * all around. (12 sts) Sl st in 1st st of this rnd.

Fasten off, and weave in loose ends.

Sew 1 head onto each "Bootie", towards the front. Sew 2 eyes/buttons onto each head.

+ TRUNK

Ch2 using yarn and 3.50mm hook.

Rnd 1: 5 sc in 2nd ch from hook. (5 sts) Do not sl st in 1st sc of this rnd.

Rnd 2: Start crocheting in 1st st from the previous rnd. 1 sc in every st all around – but only through the back loop. (5 sts) Do not sl st in 1st sc of this rnd.

Rnd 3 – 5: Start crocheting in 1st st from the previous rnd. 1 sc in every st all around. (5 sts) Do not sl st in 1st sc of this rnd.

Rnd 6: Start crocheting in 1st st from the previous rnd. 1 sc in next st, 1 dc in next 2 sts, 1 sc in next 2 sts. (5 sts) Do not sl st in 1st sc of this rnd.

Rnd 7 – 8: Start crocheting in 1st st from the previous rnd. 1 sc in every st all around. (5 sts) Sl st in 1st st of this rnd.

Fasten off, and weave in loose ends.

Sew 1 trunk onto each "Head", towards the front.

+ EARS

Ch3 using yarn and 3.50mm hook.

Row 1: 7 dc in 3rd ch from hook. Turn your work. (7 sts)

Row 2: Ch2 (counts as 1st dc), 1 dc in same st. 2 dc in next st, 1 dc in next st, 2 dc in next st, 1 dc in next st, 2 dc in next 2 sts. Turn your work. (12 sts)

Fasten off, and weave in loose ends.

Crochet 2 pairs of ears, then sew 2 ears onto each "Head", on either side of the trunk, making sure to space them out evenly.

Sweet Crochet Mary Jane Baby Shoes

Crochet HookI/9 or 5.5 mm hook

Yarn Weight(4) Medium Weight/Worsted Weight and Aran (16-20 stitches to 4 inches)

Crochet Gauge Using two strands of yarn and sc: 13 stitches and 14 rows = 4"

Finished Size Newborn - 12 Months

Materials List

Red Heart Soft Touch or Caron Simply Soft yarn (See sizes for amount required)

5.5 mm (I-9) crochet hook

Yarn needle for weaving in ends

Crochet toys, clothing, and more for baby with these free crochet patterns for the little ones:

Free Mary Jane Baby Shoe Pattern

Notes, Special Stitches, and Techniques:

Notes:

-Pattern is worked with two strands of yarn held together unless instructed otherwise

-Rounds are not joined; when you get to the end of one round continue with the next one

Invisible Join for SC or HDC: Weave the yarn tail under both loops of the second stitch to the left, then back through the center of the last stitch made. Pull the tail just tight enough so that it looks like the other stitches.

87

88

1. **Slip Stitching the Soles Together:** Place one of each color of sole together with wrong sides facing and your accent color on top, making sure to line up the stitches. With two strands of your main color, slip stitch through both layers of stitches from the last round.

2. **Invisible Join for SLIP STITCH**: Weave the yarn tail under both loops

of the starting slip stitch, and then back through the center of the last slip stitch made. Pull the tail just tight enough so that it looks like the other stitches. This counts as the last stitch of the round here and throughout the rest of the pattern.

90

91

3. **Locating the starting stitch for Round 1 of Upper:** Locate the center of the heel by laying a hook or needle along the foundation chain of the sole. It should point between two stitches. Starting with the one to the right, count 6 stitches from the center and attach your main color under both loops by making a slip stitch. Make the first sc of Round 1 in the next stitch. When you get to the end of the round, make the last sc in the same space as your starting slip stitch.

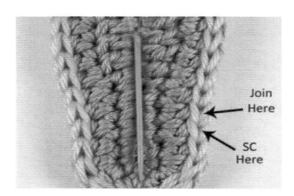

4. **Attaching the strap**: When you slip stitch the strap to the opposite side of the shoe, insert your hook from the outside of the stitch, then yarn over and pull through.

Sweet Baby Mary Jane Baby Booties:

Newborn (3.25" Length) - Requires approximately 36g (68m) of yarn.

Sole: (Make 4 – 2 of each color)

Round 1: Ch 8, make 2 sc in 2nd ch from hook, sc 2, hdc 1, dc 2, make 7 dc in last ch, working other side of chain - dc 2, hdc 1, sc 3, do not join (20)

Round 2: Make 2 sc in first 2 stitches, sc 6, *2sc* 5 times, sc 6, make 2 sc in last stitch, make an invisible join; weave in ends (28) — Slip stitch soles together.

1. **Upper:**
2. Attach main color in the 6th sl st from the center of the heel and make the first sc of Round 1 in the next sl st.
3. **Round 1:** Sc 1, hdc 8, sc 5, hdc 10, sc 4, do not join (28)
4. **Round 2:** Sc 1, hdc 8, sc 4, hdc 1, hdc2tog, *dc2tog* 3 times, hdc2tog, hdc 1, sc 3 (23)

5. **Round 3:** Sc 12, hdc 1, hdc2tog, *dc2tog* 2 times, hdc2tog, hdc 1, sc 1 (19)
6. **Round 4:** Sl st 1, sc2tog, sc 5, sc2tog, sl st 3, ch 5, skip 5 stitches and sl st in 6th stitch, make an invisible join; weave in ends
7. **0 - 3 Months** (3.75" Length) - Requires approximately 44g (84m) of yarn.
8.

9. **Sole**: (Make 4 – 2 of each color)

10. **Round 1**: Ch 9, make 2 sc in 2nd ch from hook, sc 3, hdc 1, dc 2, make 7 dc in last ch, working other side of chain - dc 2, hdc 1, sc 4, do not join (22)

11. **Round 2**: Make 2 hdc in first 2 stitches, hdc 7, *2hdc* 5 times, hdc 7, make 2 hdc in last stitch, make an invisible join; weave in ends (30) – Slip stitch soles together.

12.

13. **Upper**:

14. Attach main color in the 6th sl st from the center of the heel and make the first sc of Round 1 in the next sl st.

15. **Round 1**: Sc 1, hdc 8, sc 5, hdc 1, dc 10, hdc 1, sc 4, do not join (30)

94

16. **Round 2**: Sc 1, hdc 8, sc 5, hdc 1, hdc2tog, *dc2tog* 3 times, hdc2tog, hdc 1, sc 4 (25)

17. **Round 3**: Sc 13, hdc 1, *dc2tog* 4 times, hdc 1, sc 2 (21)

18. **Round 4**: Sl st 1, sc2tog, sc 5, sc2tog, sl st 3, ch 6, skip 6 stitches and sl st in 7th stitch, sl st 1, make an invisible join; weave in ends

19. **3 - 6 Months** (4" Length) - Requires approximately 50g (95m) of yarn.

20.

21. **Sole**: (Make 4 – 2 of each color)

22. **Round 1**: Ch 10, make 2 sc in 2nd ch from hook, sc 3, hdc 1, dc 3, make 7 dc in last ch, working other side of chain - dc 3, hdc 1, sc 4, do not join (24)

23. **Round 2**: Make 2 hdc in first 2 stitches, hdc 8, *2hdc* 5 times, hdc 8, make 2 hdc in last stitch, make an invisible join; weave in ends (32) – Slip stitch soles together.

24.

25. **Upper**:

26. Attach main color in the 6th sl st from the center of the heel and make the first sc of Round 1 in the next sl st.

27. **Round 1**: Sc 1, hdc 8, sc 6, hdc 1, dc 10, hdc 1, sc 5, do not join (32)

28. **Round 2**: Sc 1, hdc 8, sc 6, hdc 1, hdc2tog, *dc2tog* 3 times, hdc2tog, hdc 1, sc 5 (27)

29. **Round 3**: Sc 2, hdc 8, sc 4, hdc 1, *dc2tog* 4 times, hdc 1, sc 3 (23)

30. **Round 4**: Sl st 1, sc2tog, sc 5, sc2tog, sl st 4, ch 6, skip 6 stitches and sl st in 7th stitch, sl st 1, make an invisible join; weave in ends

31. **6 - 9 Months** (4.25" Length) - Requires approximately 54g (102m) of yarn.

32.

33. **Sole**: (Make 4 – 2 of each color)

34. **Round 1**: Ch 11, make 2 sc in 2nd ch from hook, sc 4, hdc 1, dc 3, make 7 dc in last ch, working other side of chain - dc 3, hdc 1, sc 5, do not join (26)

35. **Round 2**: Make 2 hdc in first 2 stitches, hdc 9, *2hdc* 5 times, hdc 9, make 2 hdc in last stitch, make an invisible join; weave in ends (34) – Slip stitch soles together.

36.

37. **Upper**:

38. Attach main color in the 6th sl st from the center of the heel and make the first sc of Round 1 in the next sl st.

39. **Round 1**: Sc 1, hdc 15, dc 12, hdc 6, do not join (34)

96

40. **Round 2**: Hdc 9, sc 6, hdc 2, hdc2tog, *dc2tog* 3 times, hdc2tog, hdc 2, sc 5 (29)

41. **Round 3**: Sc 2, hdc 8, sc 5, hdc 1, *dc2tog* 4 times, hdc 1, sc 4 (25)

42. **Round 4**: Sc2tog, hdc 7, sc2tog, sl st 4, ch 7, sk 7 stitches and sl st in 8th, sl st 2, make an invisible join; weave in ends

43. **9 - 12 Months** (4.5" Length) - Requires approximately 58g (110m) of yarn.

44.

45. **Sole**: (Make 4 – 2 of each color)

46. **Round 1**: Ch 12, make 2 sc in 2nd ch from hook, sc 4, hdc 1, dc 4, make 7 dc in last ch, working other side of chain - dc 4, hdc 1, sc 5, do not join (28)

47. **Round 2**: Make 2 hdc in first 2 stitches, hdc 10, *2hdc* 5 times, hdc 10, make 2 hdc in last stitch, make an invisible join; weave in ends (36) – Slip stitch soles together.

48.

49. **Upper**:

50. Attach main color in the 6th sl st from the center of the heel and make the first sc of Round 1 in the next sl st.

51. **Round 1**: Sc 1, hdc 16, dc 12, hdc 7, do not join (36)

52. **Round 2**: Hdc 9, sc 7, hdc 1, dc 1, *dc2tog* 5 times, dc 1, hdc 1, sc 6 (31)

53. **Round 3**: Sc 2, hdc 8, sc 6, hdc 1, *dc2tog* 4 times, hdc 1, sc 5 (27)

54. **Round 4**: Sc2tog, hdc 7, sc2tog, sl st 5, ch 7, sk 7 stitches and sl st in 8th, sl st 3, make an invisible join; weave in ends